21st Century Skills Library

REAL WORLD MATH: SPORTS

SPEED SKATING

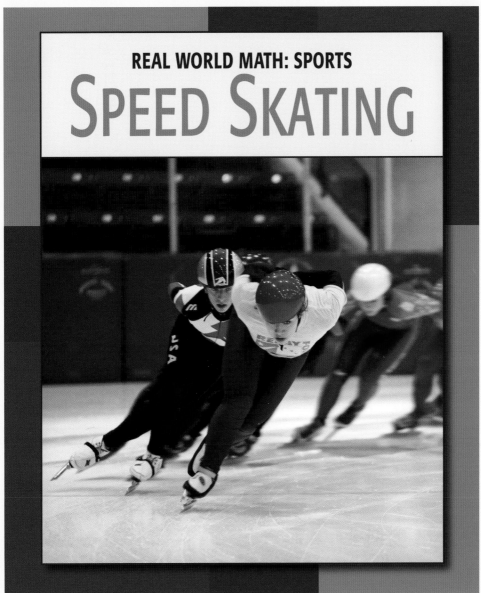

Katie Marsico and Cecilia Minden

Cherry Lake Publishing
Ann Arbor, Michigan

Published in the United States of America by Cherry Lake Publishing
Ann Arbor, Michigan
www.cherrylakepublishing.com

Math Adviser: Tonya Walker, MA, Boston University

Content Adviser: Thomas Sawyer, EdD, Professor of Recreation and Sport Management,
Indiana State University

Photo Credits: Cover and page 1, ©Jim West/Alamy; page 4, ©devi, used under license
from Shutterstock, Inc.; page 6, ©0399778584, used under license from Shutterstock,
Inc.; pages 8 and 11, ©Wally Bauman/Alamy; page 13, ©Krebs Hanns/Alamy; page 15,
©AP Photo/Ron Heflin; page 18, ©AP Photo/Jens Meyer; page 21, ©WizData, Inc., used
under license from Shutterstock, Inc.; page 25, ©Csaba Peterdi, used under license from
Shutterstock, Inc.; page 27, ©Paul Clarke, used under license from Shutterstock, Inc.

Library of Congress Cataloging-in-Publication Data
Marsico, Katie, 1980–
 Speed skating / by Katie Marsico and Cecilia Minden.
   p. cm.—(Real world math)
 Includes index.
 ISBN-13: 978-1-60279-250-0
 ISBN-10: 1-60279-250-X
 1. Speed skating—Juvenile literature. 2. Arithmetic—Juvenile
literature. I. Minden, Cecilia. II. Title. III. Series.
 GV850.3.M37 2009
 796.91'4—dc22   2008000806

Cherry Lake Publishing would like to acknowledge the work of
The Partnership for 21st Century Skills.
Please visit www.21stcenturyskills.org *for more information.*

TABLE of CONTENTS

CHAPTER ONE

Rule the Rink!   4

CHAPTER TWO

A Few Speed Skating Basics   8

CHAPTER THREE

Do the Math: Impressive Pros   15

CHAPTER FOUR

Do the Math: Remarkable Speed Skating Records   21

CHAPTER FIVE

Get Your Own Skate Going!   25

Real World Math Challenge Answers   29

Glossary   30

For More Information   31

Index   32

About the Authors   32

RULE THE RINK!

Speed skating is an exciting sport filled with many close finishes.

You hear the sound of the other skater's blades chopping at the ice behind you. You know she is close on your heels. You do not have much farther to go. Every second counts! You stay crouched down and keep your left arm over your back. One final push forward sends you speeding past the finish line. You are the champion of the match!

There is no question that you are amazing on the ice. It is not easy to master such balance and speed. Was athletic talent all that helped you win today? Absolutely not! Math skills were also important for your success

in the rink.

REAL WORLD MATH CHALLENGE

Frank and Juan are skating in a 500-meter match. Frank completes the event with a time of 56.13. That means he skated 500 meters in 56 seconds and 13 **centiseconds**. Juan finishes the event with a time of 58.10. **How many centiseconds does Frank clock in at? How about Juan? What is the difference in their times?** Remember that there are 100 centiseconds in a second.

(Turn to page 29 for the answers)

What does math have to do with speed skating? First, you should learn

a little bit about the history of the sport. Speed skating is a form of ice-

skating. Speed skaters race one another. They are focused on moving quickly.

When did skaters first take to the ice? People in Europe may have been

wearing skates as early as 10,000 years ago! These skaters were not racing

though. They were simply trying to travel over frozen lakes and rivers.

Norway has a long history of ice skating. These Norwegians enjoy skating on a frozen lake in the capital city of Oslo.

They used animal bones to make their skates. The first known speed skating **competition** dates back to 1863. Racers zipped across the ice in Norway that year. Other countries soon organized world championships.

Speed skating was first featured at the Winter Olympics in 1924. The International Skating Union (ISU) oversees all types of skating across the globe. It hosts competitions known as the ISU World Cup.

A group called U.S. Speedskating (USS) oversees the sport within the United States. The USS sponsors camps and events across the country. It also trains skaters for the Olympic Games. This organization offers opportunities to skaters of different skill levels. Some are young beginners. Others are **professional** athletes.

Now you know a little about the history of speed skating. Are you ready to learn the rules of the rink? It is time to find out how math takes skaters over the finish line. Lace up your skates, bring along your calculator, and prepare to glide to the gold!

Sports played at an international level rely on collaboration. Many countries work together so that their best athletes can compete. The ISU allows the world's finest speed skaters to prove their talent at World Cup races. Eighty skating groups from all over the globe make up the ISU. Countless cultures peacefully gather to grace the ice at its yearly events.

CHAPTER TWO

A Few Speed Skating Basics

Two long-track speed skaters prepare to race. Speed skating takes good timing and math skills as well as strength, speed, and coordination.

Have you ever skated before? It is not as easy as it looks. Skaters must have balance and speed. They also must know about measurements and math.

There are many types of speed skating competitions. The measurements and rules change for each of these competitions. Long-track rinks are oval shaped and have a 400-meter (437 yard)

circumference. These rinks can be indoor or outdoor.

However, most long-track races occur outdoors.

Long-track skaters compete in pairs. Each skater

uses a separate lane. The lanes are about 4 meters

(13 feet) wide. It may seem like the skater in the

inner lane has an unfair advantage. That is why no

one skater uses the inner lane the entire race. They

change lanes once per lap during the skate. That way,

both skaters skate the same distance.

Distances for long-track events vary. Men's races

cover 500 meters, 1,000 meters, 1,500 meters, 5,000

meters, and 10,000 meters. Women's races cover 500

Learning & Innovation Skills

Innovation has shaped the history of every major sport. Skating is no exception! Imagine what speed skaters would do if someone had not been creative enough to design an artificial ice rink. John Gamgee opened the Glaciarium in London in 1876. It was the world's first mechanically frozen ice rink.

Where would you skate if you could not visit a rink? Where would Olympic skaters go? It would not be easy or safe to host Olympic events on a frozen lake!

meters, 1,000 meters, 1,500 meters, 3,000 meters, and 5,000 meters. Most

events are skated once. Only one race is skated twice: the 500-meter race.

Judges look at a skater's total time for both races.

REAL WORLD MATH CHALLENGE

Leah races in 1,000-meter long-track events. Anna competes in 3,000-meter long-track races. So far, Leah has skated in four 1,000-meter events. Anna has participated in three 3,000-meter races. Both Leah and Anna want to skate 10,000 meters by the end of the year. **Which girl has skated farther? How much farther? What percentage of this goal has each skated up to this point?**

(Turn to page 29 for the answers)

Though skaters compete in pairs, they are racing against all other

skaters' times. The skater with the best overall time is the champion for

that event.

Skaters finish a lap when they travel all the way around the rink. They

skate in a **counterclockwise** path. They must make turns without falling

down. Skaters also must

round curves without

slowing down. They crouch

forward. They often stretch

their left arm over their

back. This gives skaters

greater speed and balance.

A skater puts his left arm behind him to increase speed and improve balance. A hooded racing suit helps make him faster, too.

Skaters' clothes help, as well. Speed skaters wear tight racing suits that

have hoods. The suits are often made from a lightweight material called

spandex. Speed skaters cannot afford to be slowed down by heavy material.

Some skaters also wear goggles. The goggles protect their eyes from wind

and flying bits of ice. How do judges tell skaters apart as they zip around

the rink? Racers wear different colored armbands. Skaters who begin racing in the inner lane usually wear white. Skaters who begin in the outer lane often wear red.

What about the most important part of a speed skater's uniform? Speed skates look like leather shoes with long, straight blades on the bottom. These metal blades usually measure between 42 and 46 centimeters (16.5 and 18 inches) long. They have a width of about 0.08 to 0.15 centimeters (0.03 to 0.06 in). Sometimes the blades are not attached at the heel. This gives speed skaters greater flexibility.

Speed skaters may be part of a team or club. Such teams and clubs often represent entire countries. For example, the U.S. National Long Track Team competes at the Winter Olympics. Professional speed skating events usually do not rely on a team scoring system though. This means that no single country is typically declared a champion in Olympic speed skating

Racers wear skates with long, sharp blades.

competitions. The exception is for team-pursuit races. These races include

two teams of three skaters each. Women's teams race six laps. Men's teams

race eight laps.

Olympic officials focus more on the performances of individual

skaters. Officials use stopwatches, digital cameras, and computers to track

racers' progress. Skaters' times are often measured in minutes, seconds,

and centiseconds. There are 100 centiseconds in a second.

Speed skating races do not last an exact time. A 500-meter event might take several seconds. A 10,000-meter race usually lasts more than 10 minutes. Races end when every athlete crosses the finish line.

Even the fastest speed skater must follow certain rules. Several rules have to do with measurements and timing. Some are related to skaters' behavior. Skaters take off when they hear the sound of an electronic starting pistol. Racers cannot begin skating before the starting pistol is fired. They have to be careful not to touch other skaters. They must stay in their own lane and switch over at the right time. Judges decide if a skater has broken a rule. Too many broken rules can disqualify a skater from an event.

Does all this sound like a lot to remember? Being comfortable with numbers and measurements will help guide you around the rink. Math skills will give you what it takes to become a champion on the ice!

CHAPTER THREE

DO THE MATH:
IMPRESSIVE PROS

Olympic gold medalist Dan Jansen
wipes the ice off his skates after a race.

What does it take

to become a champion

speed skater? These

athletes must have speed

and **endurance**. They

must also be determined

and dedicated. U.S.

skater Dan Jansen

possessed all these

qualities. He began competing in the Winter Olympics in 1984. His fans

believed he would win the gold in 1988. They were certain he would lead

in the men's 500-meter and 1,000-meter races. But

that did not happen.

The skating star received tragic news shortly

before the 500-meter event at the 1988 Olympics.

He learned his sister had just died of cancer. His

performance on the ice suffered during the next few

days. He fell during both races and failed to finish.

Jansen kept pushing hard though. Over the next few

years, he proved his talent during ISU World Cup

competitions. He never gave up on the idea that he

could and would win the Olympic gold.

The 1994 Winter Olympics was Jansen's moment

to shine. He came in first in the men's 1,000-meter

event and won the gold medal. He also achieved a world-record time of 1:12.43! He retired later that year. Other speed skaters have since broken his record, but his story will never be forgotten. Jansen was determined to skate his way to the top. His attitude was as important to his success as his talent.

Many famous speed skaters have made their mark on the ice. Claudia Pechstein is an impressive German skater. Pechstein claimed nine Olympic medals between 1992 and 2006! Five were gold. She won in both the

REAL WORLD MATH CHALLENGE

Finnish skater Pekka Koskela currently holds the world record for the men's 1,000-meter race. He clocked in at 1:7.0 in 2007. He beat the previous record by Shani Davis, which was recorded at 1:7.3 in 2005. **How many total centiseconds did it take him to finish his skate? How many more centiseconds did it take Davis?** Remember that there are 60 seconds in 1 minute, and 100 centiseconds in one second.

(Turn to page 29 for the answers)

Claudia Pechstein of Germany (middle) races during a women's team pursuit in 2007. In this event, two teams of three skaters compete at a time.

women's 3,000-meter and 5,000-meter races. She also won a women's team

pursuit in 2006.

Pechstein is the first female athlete in the Winter Olympics to earn

five **consecutive** medals. This means that she won medals in five Winter

Olympics in a row. She currently holds two Olympic records. One is for her incredible time in the women's 3,000-meter race in 2002. She clocked in at 3:57.70. The other Olympic record is for her 2002 performance in the women's 5,000-meter race. Pechstein finished that event in 6:46.91.

Her role in the 2005 World Championship women's team resulted in a world record. Pechstein and two other teammates completed six laps in 2:56.40. This remarkable athlete has yet to retire. She will surely cross the finish line at more record-setting times in the years ahead.

Speed skaters are honored for their talent on the ice in many ways. Some are awarded trophies and medals. Others are named Speed Skater of the Year. A few, such as Jansen, are welcomed into the U.S. Olympic Hall of Fame. Most awards are divided up according to distances skated. Numbers make up a huge part of a skater's success. A skater's numbers in turn win them fans and fame.

Speed skaters often claim prize money when they perform well in a race. Some athletes use this money to help others. This was true for U.S. speed skater Joey Cheek. He won $25,000 in prize money when he claimed the gold in the 2006 Winter Olympics. Cheek won the men's 500-meter race. He used his prize money to aid people in a war-torn area in Africa called Darfur.

REAL WORLD MATH CHALLENGE

Joey Cheek claimed his first Olympic gold medal at the Turin Winter Olympic Games in 2006. He won the 500-meter race with a time of 1:09.76. Silver medalist and runner up, Dmitry Dorofeyev, clocked in at 1:10.41. **What was the difference between these two times?** Remember, there are 60 seconds in 1 minute.

(Turn to page 29 for the answer)

CHAPTER FOUR

Do the Math: Remarkable Speed Skating Records

Can you imagine flying around an ice rink at about 30 miles (48 kilometers) per hour? That is how fast some speed skaters move. They are always trying to improve their times and set new records. Canadian speed skater

Setting speed-skating records takes hours of training.

Cindy Klassen currently holds three world records in her sport.

Klassen boasts record times for the women's 1,000-meter, 1,500-meter, and 3,000-meter events. It took her only 1:51.79 to complete the 1,500-meter event in 2005. She clocked in at 3:53.34 in the 3,000-meter race in 2006, and wowed fans when she finished the 1,000-meter skate in 1:13.11 in that same year. She now holds the greatest number of current world records in women's speed skating.

U.S. speed skater Shani Davis has set world records in the men's 1,500-meter event. In 2007, his time was 1:42.32.

REAL WORLD MATH CHALLENGE

In 2005, Cindy Klassen finished her 1,500-meter event in 1:51.79. In 2007, Shani Davis skated the same distance for the men's race in 1:42.32. **How many total centiseconds did the skate take Klassen? How about Davis? What is the average of the skaters' times?**

(Turn to page 29 for the answers)

Davis is tied with Dutch speed skater Sven Kramer for his number of world records. Kramer set amazing times in the 5,000-meter and 10,000-meter events in 2007. He completed the shorter race in 6:3.32. He finished the longer skate with a time of 12:41.69.

Some speed skaters have earned records for more than just speed.

Famous skater Bonnie Blair holds the record for most Winter Olympic medals won by an American woman. She claimed the gold five times between 1988 and 1994. Three medals were for women's 500-meter events. Two were for women's 1,000-meter events. Blair also took home a bronze medal for the women's 1,000-meter race in 1988.

Other U.S. skaters have made their mark at the Olympics. Two American speed skaters currently hold two Olympic records for their country. U.S. athletes have set top times in the Olympic men's 500-meter skate and the 1,500-meter event.

Many Olympic speed skaters also set ISU World Cup records. Pechstein, Klassen, Davis, and Kramer all hold current records for ISU competitions.

Speed skaters who hope to win the Olympic gold need to have strong motivation to win. Blair is a perfect example. She was determined to make it to the top. She began skating when she was just four years old! She was only 19 when she joined the U.S. Olympic team in 1984. Blair retired in 1995. She was welcomed into the U.S. Olympic Hall of Fame in 2004. Her drive and talent made her one of the most successful female athletes in the Olympic Games.

Do you see how numbers can make speed skaters unforgettable champs? Skaters try to improve their times during every event. They hope to grow faster with each skate. This is why so many speed skating fans like watching races. A skater could break old records every time he hits the ice. Maybe someday you will be the star who rules the rink!

REAL WORLD MATH CHALLENGE

Bonnie Blair won the gold 5 times. She claimed 3 medals for women's 500-meter events. She took home 2 gold medals for women's 1,000-meter skates. **How many total meters did Blair skate during races that resulted in Olympic gold medals?**

(Turn to page 29 for the answer)

CHAPTER FIVE

GET YOUR OWN SKATE GOING!

For beginners, skating lessons at a nearby rink are a great place to start.

Do you have to be a professional speed skater to enjoy the ice?

Absolutely not! Maybe you would like to learn how to race around the

rink. You can check with your local rink or community center to see if they

offer speed skating lessons. They might even have a competitive club you

can join.

Maybe you prefer just skating with your friends. You do not have to

race anyone to have a good time. Ice-skating is also an excellent way to get

exercise during winter. Many towns have public rinks. Some are outside.

Others are indoors. These rinks often offer skate rentals for a small fee.

REAL WORLD MATH CHALLENGE

Carl and four of his friends want to go ice-skating at the town rink. Skate rental is $5 per pair. **How many pairs of skates will the group need? What will be the total cost?**

(Turn to page 29 for the answers)

Maybe you would rather buy your own skates. Keep in mind that there

are different types. Certain skates are built for speed. Others are designed

for grace on the ice. The skates you rent from a local rink will probably be

most similar to figure skates. These skates help figure skaters leap and twirl.

You have already learned that speed skaters use skates that allow them to be quick and flexible. Talk to the staff at

a sports store to see what skate is best

for you, if you want to buy your own.

What else should you wear if

you decide to visit the rink with

your friends? You will want to pick

clothes that will help you stay warm.

A lot of people choose sweaters or

long-sleeved shirts. They dress in

Remember to wear
warm clothing when
you take to the ice.

sweatpants or exercise pants. Many skaters also have earmuffs, knit hats,

and gloves. Be sure to wear warm socks.

Do you need any extra protection in case you slip? Some skaters wear

helmets and special pads on their knees, elbows, and wrists. It is important

21st Century Content

There is more to good health than exercise. Speed skating stars must eat a balanced diet. The Food Pyramid shows how much people should eat from each food group. Sleep is also important. Experts say that many Olympic athletes need eight to nine hours of sleep a night. Would you have guessed that going to bed on time could improve your performance on the ice?

to be careful on the ice. Never push other skaters. Always look ahead so you do not run into anyone in front of you. Also, check to see if your local rink has any special rules.

Is it taking you awhile to get used to ice-skating? Don't be frustrated if you are not racing across the rink just yet. Remember that even Olympic winners had to start somewhere. Keep in mind that your math skills will also help you as you push to become the next speed skating champion. You have practiced addition, subtraction, multiplication, and division. Now get set to skate to victory!

REAL WORLD MATH CHALLENGE ANSWERS

Chapter One
Page 5

Frank clocks in at 5,613 centiseconds.

56 seconds x 100 centiseconds = 5,600 centiseconds

5,600 centiseconds + 13 centiseconds = 5,613 centiseconds

Juan finishes in 5,810 centiseconds.

58 seconds x 100 centiseconds = 5,800 centiseconds

5,800 centiseconds + 10 centiseconds = 5,810 centiseconds

There is a difference of 197 centiseconds in their times.

5,810 centiseconds − 5,613 centiseconds = 197 centiseconds

Chapter Two
Page 10

Leah has skated 4,000 meters so far.

4 races x 1,000 meters = 4,000 meters

Anna has skated 9,000 meters up to this point.

3 races x 3,000 meters = 9,000 meters

Anna has skated 5,000 meters farther.

9,000 meters − 4,000 meters = 5,000 meters

Leah has skated 40 percent of her goal.

4,000 meters ÷ 10,000 meters = 0.40 = 40%

Anna has skated 90 percent of her goal.

9,000 meters ÷ 10,000 meters = 0.90 = 90%

Chapter Three
Page 17

It took Koskela 6,700 centiseconds to finish his race.

1 minute x 60 seconds = 60 seconds

60 seconds + 7 seconds = 67 seconds

67 seconds x 100 centiseconds = 6,700 centiseconds

It took Davis 6,703 centiseconds to finish his race.

1 minute x 60 seconds = 60 seconds

60 seconds + 7 seconds = 67 seconds

67 seconds x 100 centiseconds = 6,700 centiseconds

6,700 centiseconds + 3 centiseconds = 6,703 centiseconds

It took Davis 3 centiseconds longer to finish the race.

6,703 − 6,700 = 3 centiseconds

Page 20

Cheek's time was 1: 09.76. Dorofeyev's time was 1:10.41.

1:09.76 = 60 seconds + 9 seconds +0.76 seconds = 69.76 seconds

1:10.41 = 60 seconds + 10 seconds + 0.41 seconds = 70.41 seconds

70.41 seconds - 69.76 seconds = 0.65 second

The difference between the skaters' times was 0.65 second, or 65 centiseconds.

Chapter Four
Page 22

The event took Klassen 11,179 centiseconds.

1 minute x 60 seconds = 60 seconds

60 seconds + 51 seconds = 111 seconds

111 seconds x 100 centiseconds = 11,100 centiseconds

11,100 centiseconds + 79 centiseconds = 11,179 centiseconds

Davis finished his race in 10,232 centiseconds.

1 minute x 60 seconds = 60 seconds

60 seconds + 42 seconds = 102 seconds

102 seconds x 100 centiseconds = 10,200 centiseconds

10,200 centiseconds + 32 centiseconds = 10,232 centiseconds

The average of their times is 10,706 centiseconds.

11,179 + 10,232 = 21,411

21,411 ÷ 2 = 10,705.5 = 10,706 centiseconds

Page 24

Blair skated a total of 3,500 meters during races that resulted in gold medals.

3 races x 500 meters = 1,500 meters

2 races x 1,000 meters = 2,000 meters

1,500 meters + 2,000 meters = 3,500 meters

Chapter Five
Page 26

The group will need 5 pairs of skates.

1 person (Carl) + 4 friends = 5 people = 5 pairs of skates

They will pay a total cost of $25.00.

5 pairs x $5.00 = $25.00

Glossary

centiseconds (SEN-tuh-seh-kunds) units of measurement that make up one-hundredth of a second

circumference (sir-KUM-frents) the boundary line around a circle

competition (kom-puh-TISH-uhn) a race or sporting event in which opposite players or teams attempt to outdo one another

consecutive (kuhn-SEK-yuh-tiv) back-to-back or one after another

counterclockwise (koun-tur-KLOK-wize) in a direction opposite to the one in which the hands on a clock move

endurance (in-DUR-unss) the ability to keep up intense exercise or activity over an extended period of time

professional (pruh-FESH-uh-nuhl) describing a sport that is played for money or as a career

FOR MORE INFORMATION

Books

Borden, Louise, and Niki Daly (illustrator). *The Greatest Skating Race: A World War II Story from the Netherlands*. New York: Margaret K. McElderry Books, 2004.

The U.S. Olympic Committee. *A Basic Guide to Speed Skating*. Torrance, CA: Griffin Publishing Group, 2002.

Web Sites

International Skating Union Official Site
www.isu.org/
Learn more about all kinds of skating competitions

U.S. Speedskating
www.usspeedskating.org/
For the U.S. speed skating team's latest news and biographies

Index

armbands, 11–12

balance, 4, 8, 11
blades, 12
Blair, Bonnie, 23, 24

centiseconds, 5, 13, 17, 22
Cheek, Joey, 20
circumference, 9
clothing, 11, 27
clubs, 12, 25
collaboration, 7
competitions, 4, 6, 8, 12–13, 16, 23
computers, 13
curves, 11

Davis, Shani, 17, 22, 23
digital cameras, 13
disqualifications, 14
distances, 9–10, 19

endurance, 15

figure skating, 26
Food Pyramid, 28

Gamgee, John, 9
Glaciarium, 9
goggles, 11

history, 5–7

ice rinks. See skating rinks.
ice-skating, 5, 26, 28
International Skating Union (ISU), 6, 7, 16, 23

Jansen, Dan, 15–17, 19
judges, 10, 11, 14

Klassen, Cindy, 21–22, 23
Koskela, Pekka, 17

Kramer, Sven, 22, 23

lanes, 9, 12, 14
laps, 9, 10–11, 13
long-track rinks, 8–9, 10

measurements, 8, 12, 13, 14

Olympic Games, 6, 7, 12–13, 15–16, 17–19, 20, 23, 24, 28

Pechstein, Claudia, 17–19, 23
prize money, 20

records, 17, 18–19, 21–23, 24
rules, 8, 14, 28

safety, 9, 27–28
scoring, 12–13

skates, 5, 6, 12, 26–27
skating rinks, 8–9, 25, 26, 28
sleep, 28
spandex, 11
speed, 4, 8, 11, 21
starting pistols, 14
stopwatches, 13

team-pursuit races, 13, 18
times, 5, 10, 13, 14, 17, 19, 21–22, 24

U.S. National Long Track Team, 12
U.S. Olympic Hall of Fame, 19, 24
U.S. Speedskating (USS) group, 7

World Cup competition, 6, 7, 16, 23

About the Authors

Katie Marsico worked as a managing editor in children's publishing before becoming a freelance writer. She lives near Chicago, Illinois, with her husband and two children. She has never participated in Olympic speed skating but feels she has gained extensive experience on the ice during Chicago winters.

Cecilia Minden, PhD, is a former classroom teacher and university professor who now enjoys being an author and consultant for children's books. She lives with her family near Chapel Hill, North Carolina. She dedicates this book to her brother, Patrick, who loved to ice-skate.